All About Animals

Squirrels

By Justine Ciovacco

Reader's Digest Young Families

Contents

Chapter 1
A Squirrel Story

Who's a Rat?

Squirrels are rodents. They belong to the *Rodentia* order of mammals. Rats, mice, and porcupines are also members of this group.

Mama Squirrel is a gray tree squirrel, and she has been getting ready for winter—that means finding food and storing it away. Her babies have gone off to live on their own now, so she only needs to store enough food for herself. She has dug hundreds of holes in the ground to hide acorns and seeds.

There is a chill in the air, and Mama Squirrel knows it is time to find a new home. Winter is almost here. Mama quickly runs up and back down each tree trunk and then she races back onto the ground.

Mama spends a lot of time running up, down, and around one giant oak tree. She feels every inch of it with her paws and whiskers. Soon Mama finds an empty hole. She gnaws at some bark to open it up a bit. Then she sticks her head inside. It seems safe. She rubs her face around the hole and spreads her saliva around to mark it with her scent. This spot belongs to her!

Daddy's Not Home

Father tree squirrels do not raise their young. Mothers must find food and care for their young alone.

Then Mama climbs back down the tree. She hunts for leaves, grass, feathers, and fur on the ground. She uses her mouth to carry them in bunches back to her new home. She also continues to find and store acorns, seeds, and any other food she can find. She does this until it begins to snow. Then she only comes out of her warm nest every few days to look for her buried food.

After a few months, the weather gets warmer and the ground gets softer. It is spring. Gathering food will be much easier now. Mama Squirrel is glad of that because she has to pay attention to something else now. She's going to have some new babies! Mama Squirrel begins to collect leaves and twigs for a new nest. She'll make this one on a nearby branch of the tree.

A few weeks later, Mama Squirrel goes to her nest and gives birth to four little babies. She is ready to take good care of them. As they take their first breaths of air, Mama licks their pink skin clean. She nudges each one closer to her to help them drink her milk.

The newborns are only about an inch long. Their eyes are tightly closed, and they have hardly any fur. They snuggle together to stay warm. And they snuggle close to Mama when she's in the nest. She has to leave at least once a day to find food.

After three weeks, the baby squirrels have grown quite a bit. They still cuddle, but they are bigger. Now they often push one another to the edge of the nest. Mama tries to make sure that they stay together.

One day Mama leaves the nest to go hunting. The smallest baby squirrel is pushed out of the nest. He falls to the ground with a soft *thump*. He is confused. After all, he can barely see anything. And this is not the warm leafy nest he's used to living in!

Mama comes back with a nut in her mouth. As she reaches her tree's roots, she sees a cat lying under a nearby tree. Mama thinks the cat may be watching her. She drops the nut and runs up the tree in circles to confuse the cat. She reaches her nest and sees that a baby is missing.

Mama quickly climbs down the tree. She keeps an eye on the cat. But at the same time, she sniffs all around to find her baby. She finds him in the grass. Mama quickly grabs the back of his neck with her teeth and carries him up the tree trunk. She nestles him in the midst of her other three babies.

After a month, the baby squirrels' eyes and ears begin to open. They have trouble seeing at first. And they have to get used to the sounds around them. By now, most of their fur has grown in and they drink less of Mama's milk.

One sunny day, Mama nudges her little ones and chatters to them. She is letting them know it is time for them to learn how to find and store food. But first she has to show them how to climb down the tree without getting caught by the cat. These young squirrels have a lot to learn. But Mama is ready to teach them.

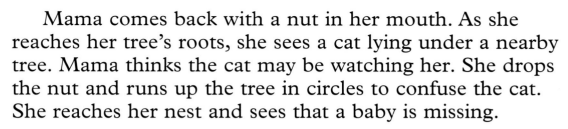

Tree Squirrel Truths

Gray squirrels are just one kind of tree squirrel. The fox squirrel is also a popular tree squirrel. It has reddish-brown fur and shares some habitats with the gray squirrel. All tree squirrels have long, bushy tails.

Chapter 2
The Body of a Squirrel

The word *squirrel* is based on
two ancient Greek words that
mean "shade tail."

Fur for All

The color of a squirrel's coat usually depends on where it lives. Gray squirrels are the most common tree squirrels in North America. They live in the eastern United States and parts of Canada. Their gray or gray-brown fur coats blend in with the bark of the native trees, especially the oak. Some gray squirrels have a reddish color mixed in with the gray. But the bellies of the gray squirrel are always white.

The color of the Douglas tree squirrels blends with the trunks of the pine trees in the Northwest. Ground squirrels like the rock squirrel and the 13-striped ground squirrel blend in with the colors of the prairies and deserts.

In the summer, tree squirrels have lightweight fur coats and thinner tails. But as winter approaches, they grow a thick extra coat of fur on their bodies and tails. This extra layer keeps them warmer and helps keep water and snow away from their skin.

A bushy tail is important to a tree squirrel. The squirrel uses its tail as a blanket to keep warm when it sleeps. A tail also works like and umbrella in rainy or snowy weather. In the summer, a bushy tail can give a squirrel some shade. Most important, a squirrel uses its tail as a balancing tool, whooshing it up, down, and sideways as it scurries along tree limbs, roofs, or utility lines.

Fancy Footwork

A squirrel's feet are very strong. Each hind foot has five toes with sharp, curved nails that make climbing easy. These powerful hind feet also make easy work of leaping from one branch to another.

Each front foot also has five toes, but one of them is very small and thumblike. This helps squirrels move and hold on to nuts and other foods as they eat them.

Whether it is climbing up a tree or down a tree, a squirrel travels head first. It keeps its head up so it can watch for the first sign of danger when it reaches the ground. Sometimes a sqirrel will run circles around the tree as it climbs up in order to confuse any predator that might be watching. After all, it's hard to catch a squirrel that's running all around a tree!

As squirrels climb, they move their back feet and front feet forward in pairs. This motion helps them get a good grip on the climbing surface, whether it is the bark of a tree or a stone wall.

Squirrels sit upright on their hind legs to rest, to eat, and to keep on the watch for predators. They keep their tail behind them for balance.

Squirrelly Swimmers?

A tree squirrel is a good swimmer. It uses its feet to paddle, and its tail acts like a boat's rudder. The tail helps the squirrel steer and balance so it can get where it wants to go.

A squirrel's feet are very strong and flexible. Squirrels can climb and hold on to surfaces that most other animals can not.

A squirrel's mouth can hold plenty of food.

Teethy Tools

Like all members of the rodent family, squirrels have long, sharp front teeth. The four front teeth, two on the bottom and two on the top, are gnawing teeth called incisors. They allow squirrels to "saw" away on the hard surfaces of nuts, seeds, and bark. The incisors wear down from gnawing. But that's not a problem for squirrels, because these teeth are always growing!

There is a big space behind the incisors. The space makes it easy for squirrels to carry nuts and other items. There are three pairs of molars, or grinding teeth, farther back on each side of the squirel's jaw. All of these molars make chewing possible.

A squirrel's jaws are perfect for the foods it enjoys eating. The lower jaw moves forward so that the upper and lower incisors meet when the squirrel bites into something. Then the squirrel moves its lower jaw back a bit so that the pairs of molars meet when the squirrel is grinding food.

Wash-and-Wear Fur Coats

Squirrels use their tongues as washcloths. They lick their front paws first and then rub the paws over their face and neck. Next, they lick their body fur and hind legs. Then they hold their tail between their paws and comb it with their teeth. Finally, they lick the tail clean. A tail is at its fluffiest when it's clean!

Seeing and Hearing

Squirrels have very good eyesight. Their eyes are set high on the sides of their head. This allows them to see all around without having to move their heads a lot. They can even see clearly in the dim light of the early evening.

Squirrels also have great hearing. Their ears are relatively large for their size. Some kinds of sqirrels have ears that are shaped like funnels. This helps them hear even soft sounds that are very far away.

Smelling

Squirrels have an excellent sense of smell—and it's a good thing that they do. Why? Because they have a terrible memory. If it weren't for their sense of smell, squirrels would probably starve.

When a tree squirrel finds a nut, it quickly looks for a safe spot to hide it. It may tuck the nut into a tiny hole or crack in a tree limb. Or it may dig a hole about an inch deep at the base of a tree. Then it will drop in the nut and cover the hole with dirt. Squirrels hide their nuts one by one, and in a different place each time. But they don't remember where they hid their treasures. Squirrels use their excellent sense of smell to help them find the hidden food. They can even smell nuts under a foot of snow!

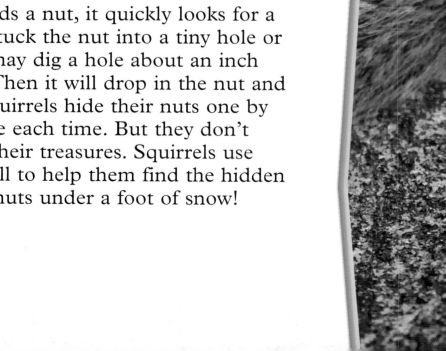

Squirrels often hide nuts near tree roots that are coated with the squirrel's saliva. The smell of their own saliva helps atract them to the right hiding place.

Squirrel Talk

Tree squirrels communicate with each other by a series of chirps. Scientists believe the tone of the chirp and how long it lasts indicate different messages. Some chirps warn of danger, while others are a kind of laughter.

Chapter 3
How Squirrels Survive

I'll Be Back
When squirrels leave their nests, they wipe their saliva against the nearby branches to let other animals know that they have been there—and will probably return.

Squirrels often find safety and warmth in the feeders that people put out for birds.

Safe at Home

In spring and summer, tree squirrels usually build nests called dreys on a tree's high branches. The squirrels use their mouths to carry leaves, pine needles, twigs, and other "building materials" from the ground to a spot where many branches come together. This gives the nest a safe and steady base.

Adult tree squirrels live alone in their dreys when the weather is nice. But during a storm, a few squirrels may huddle together in one squirrel's nest to keep warm.

Tree squirrels do not hibernate, or go into a deep sleep, during the winter months, even if they live in a place where the weather gets very cold. But they do need to build a new nest where they can keep warm throughout the chilly season. When the weather gets cooler, squirrels look for holes in the trunks and thick branches of trees. The holes may have been made by woodpeckers or other birds. Squirrels make the holes bigger by chewing away the tree bark with their sharp teeth and digging at the holes with their strong claws.

Trees squirrels may stay in their winter homes for several days without leaving. They do not have to eat every day because they ate a lot and stored fat during the warmer months. Still, every few days a squirrel will climb out of its warm hole to search for some fresh food or to look for food they hid away months or days earlier.

Most ground squirrels live in burrows under the ground all through the year.

Food Run

Squirrels leave their homes mainly to find food. Sometimes they hide it away for another day. Sometimes they eat their favorite foods right where they find them or bring them back to their nests. Favorite foods include nuts, seeds, insects, fruit, mushrooms, certain types of leaves, and sometimes even eggs and small animals.

Squirrels know what to do with food, even if they are not hungry. If they find a nut, they will break the shell with their teeth. Then they clean the nut or other food by licking it or rubbing it on their face. Next, they quickly bury the food they want to store, or sometimes they hide it in a tree's cracks. They may rebury it hours or days later if they find a safer hiding place. Each squirrel may make several thousand diggings each year.

Danger Ahead!

A squirrel's constant moving around to hunt and gather food makes it an easy target for some predators. A tree squirrel's predators include cats, dogs, skunks, raccoons, hawks, snakes, and owls.

If a squirrel sees a predator, it usually "freezes" in position. It does this because then the enemy may miss seeing it. But a tree squirrel is always ready to race away, especially if a tree is nearby.

Crafty Critters

Squirrels are ready to try anything when it comes to finding food. They can often be found eating out of bird feeders and digging around plants to find seeds. Squirrels will return to the same place every day if they find it's a good source for food. That is why people often see the same squirrels in their yards.

Squirrels will hide away an ear of corn and keep coming back to it until all the kernels are gone.

Chapter 4
Special Squirrels

Chipmunks live in North America and parts of Asia. These little ground squirrels are famous for being able to stuff their cheeks with food. They do not keep it there for long because they store it in their burrows.

Groundhogs

Groundhogs, which are also known as woodchucks, are very large ground squirrels.

Groundhogs live in the eastern and central parts of the United States, in Alaska, and in the western parts of Canada.

Groundhog burrows are often very large, with many connecting tunnels.

The Family Tree

There are many different kinds of squirrels in the squirrel family. Some of them look and act alike. Others are very diffferent. There are tree squirrels, which also include flying squirrels. And there are ground squirrels, which include chipmunks, prairie dogs, and squirrels that look a lot like tree squirrels.

Ground squirrels usually live where there are no trees. Instead, they live in underground burrows. Some ground squirrels hibernate, or go into a deep sleep, during the coldest months of the year. Some ground squirrels that live in very hot areas go into a deep sleep during the hottest months.

Prairie Dogs

A prairie dog may not have a long, bushy tail, but it is a squirrel. It uses its short tail and a series of barks to "talk" to other prairie dogs.

Prairie dogs live in large family groups called colonies. Their home is an "underground town" of connected burrows. The burrows keep them cool in the heat of day and warm during the chilly nights.

As Cold As It Gets

Arctic ground squirrels live in the bushy meadows and along the rivers of Alaska and northern Canada's tundra.

For five months of each year, these squirrels battle cold rain and strong winds to find the plant foods they need. The rest of year, the weather is even colder. That's when the Arctic ground squirrels hibernate, or go into a deep sleep.

When the squirrels hibernate, their bodies become colder than ice! Their hearts beat only one or two times a minute, and they take only about three breaths a minute. They do not need much food because they are in a deep sleep. But every few weeks, they wake up and eat a small meal.

Flying Fur!

Flying squirrels are a kind of tree squirrel. Unlike other tree squirrels, they are active at night. Their big eyes help them see in the dark. These squirrels don't really fly, but they do glide from branch to branch.

Flying squirrels have wide flaps of skin along their sides. When they leap, they spread out their front and back legs, and the skin flaps spread out too. They can make the flaps tighter by turning their wrists. The tightness of the flaps helps them turn and stop as they glide. Their bodies work a lot like kites!

Flying squirrels can be found in parts of Canada, the northeastern United States, and Central America.

Happy Squirrel Day!

Every February 2, people in the United States and Canada celebrate Groundhog Day. The "legend" is that If a groundhog comes out of its burrow that day and sees its shadow, it will be frightened and will run right back inside and hibernate for another 6 weeks. That means that spring weather will be at least another 6 weeks away. But if the groundhog doesn't see its shadow, it will stay out of its burrow and go about its regular business. Spring will be early.

Arctic ground squirrels survive in the cold by digging deep holes in the ground and living in them for most of the year.

Albino squirrels are so popular in Austin, Texas that students at the University of Texas started the Albino Squirrel Preservation Society in 2001. This group thinks the albino squirrels that live on campus bring them luck on tests!

White Squirrels?

Not all gray squirrels look gray or even brownish. In fact, some gray squirrels are white!

White squirrels are white because their bodies don't produce melanin (pronounced *MEL uh nin*). Melanin is a substance produced by the body that gives color to skin and fur (or, in humans, to skin and hair). Some squirrels have so little melanin that even their eyes have no dark color. These white squirrels with pinkish eyes are called albino (pronounced *al BINE oh*) squirrels.

Marionville, Missouri has enacted special laws to protect the albino squirrels that live there. The townspeople place feeders all around so the squirrels will have plenty to eat. Other places with large albino squirrel populations include the towns of Olney, Illinois and Kenton, Tennessee.

Black Squirrels?

Black squirrels are also gray tree squirrels. Their bodies produce so much melanin that their fur is extra dark! In 1902 a group of 18 Canadian black squirrels was released at the National Zoo in Washington, DC. Today there are hundreds of them in the area. Scientists think their dark color helps them survive. In the winter, the dark coats hold more heat from the sunlight than the coats of their gray squirrel relatives.

Chapter 5
Squirrels in the World

Where Squirrels Live

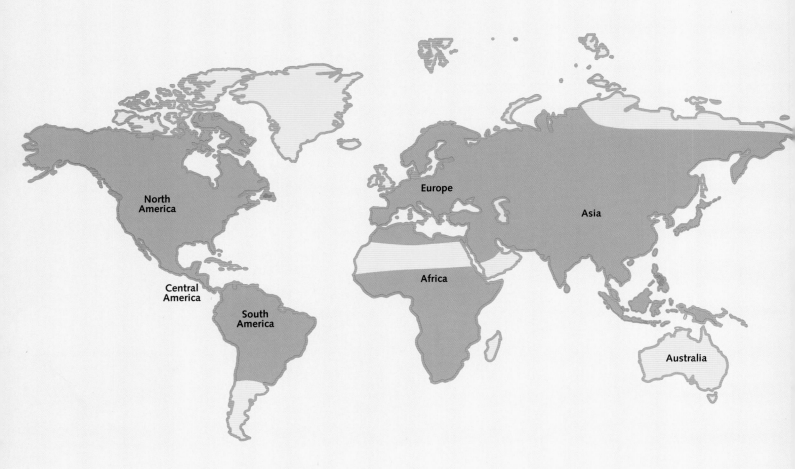

North America

Europe

Asia

Central America

Africa

South America

Australia

The **green** areas show where squirrels live.

Squirrels Everywhere!

There are more than 300 different species, or kinds, of squirrels in the world. Some live in wide open grasslands and prairies, and some live in forests thick with trees. Other squirrels survive in hot deserts and muggy rain forests, while still others burrow into the cold, hard ground of the Arctic tundra.

Squirrels can be found in almost every part of the world except Antarctica, Australia, Madagascar, Polynesia, and the southern part of South America. They are able to live in so many places because each kind of squirrel has adapted, or changed, so that it can survive and thrive in its specific habitat.

Tree squirrels live in places that have lots of trees and where the weather is not very cold for most of the year. Many kinds of tree squirrrels can be found in parts of North and South America, Europe, and Asia.

No Babysitting Allowed!

If a baby squirrel falls from its nest in your yard, don't go too close to it or touch it. Watch from a distance. Usually its mother will find it and carry it home. If she doesn't show up in a couple of hours, call a local animal rescue group. They know just what to do.

The Future of Squirrels

Squirrels are among the most adaptable of all mammals, which is why there are so many squirrels in the world today. Today's squirrels have been able to adapt to the changes in their surroundings. Gray tree squirrels are as comfortable living in city parks and suburban backyards and climbing along utility lines as they are living in forests of oak trees.

But adapting is not always easy. Squirrels in North America were once hunted by Native Americans and, later, by the early European settlers as food and for their fur. Farmers used to kill them because they ate their crops. Squirrel hunting is still a popular and legal sport in many states.

People are the cause of many problems for tree squirrels. Tree squirrels often lose their homes and food sources when trees are cut down to clear land. And wherever there are roads for squirrels to cross, there are always cars that may hit them by accident.

Fast Facts About Gray Squirrels

Scientific name	*Sciurus carolinensis*
Class	Mammalia
Order	Rodentia
Size	Up to 15 inches long
Weight	Up to 1 pound
Life span	Six years
Habitat	Forests, parks, backyards

Hit or Miss

Many squirrels die before they reach their first birthday. They are most often hit and killed by cars. When a squirrel sees a car coming, it will run in circles and in all different directions. The squirrel thinks this movement will confuse the oncoming car and make it go in a different direction. Of course, this action most often makes the squirrel harder to avoid hitting.

The red squirrel is one of the most common squirrels in North America.

Glossary of Wild Words

burrow   a ground squirrel's tunnellike underground home

communicate   to exchange thoughts, feelings, and information through signs and sounds

den   a tree squirrel's winter home, usually inside a tree

drey   a tree squirrel's nest built on the branches of a tree

gnaw   to bite or chew with the teeth

habitat   the natural environment where an animal or plant lives

hibernate   to go into a deep sleep all winter

incisors   long, sharp teeth that help an animal bite into things

ammal   an animal with a backbone and hair on its body that drinks milk from its mother when it is born

elanin   a substance produced by the body that gives color to the skin and fur or hair of an animal

olars   broad, flat teeth in the back of the mouth used for grinding

edator   an animal that hunts and eats other animals to survive

dent   a small mammal with a single pair of sharp incisors in each jaw

saliva   the watery liquid produced in an animal's mouth

species   a group of plants or animals that are the same in many ways

tundra   an area without trees in an Arctic region with short plants and a frozen layer of soil underground

woodchuck   another name for a groundhog

Index